# Pause.

Your Body Is Trying To Tell You Something

Leigha Briolo

Pause.

Your Body Has Been Trying to Tell You Something.

*A Guide to Coherence, Emotional Regulation, and Self-Trust*

© 2026 by **Leigha Briolo**

**Disclaimer**

This book is intended for educational and informational purposes only. It is not a substitute for professional medical, psychological, psychiatric, or therapeutic advice, diagnosis, or treatment.

The practices and reflections in this book are designed to support self-awareness, emotional regulation, and personal growth. Readers are encouraged to seek qualified professional support when needed and to use their own judgement and care when applying the material.

Published by **Remembering Press**
First edition
Printed in the United States of America

ISBN: 979-8-9944074-0-0

*You were born into a system that never taught you how to remember yourself – only how to forget.*

There is a moment, quiet and almost invisible, when the heart speaks before the mind catches up.

We feel it as a pull, a knowing, a steady rhythm beneath the chaos. Some call it intuition. Some call it instinct. Science calls it coherence.

But coherence is more than a concept—it is the forgotten language of the body.

It is the place where clarity lives.
The place where truth lives.
The place where you finally hear yourself.

For years we've been taught to trust the mind above all else.
But the mind is loud.
The mind reacts.
The mind protects.

The heart informs.
The heart remembers.
The heart leads.

This book is not simply about the mechanics of heart and brain communication.

It's about returning to the part of you that has never been lost.

It is about awakening the intelligence that exists beneath fear, beneath doubt, beneath every story you were told about who you are.

Coherence is not something you learn.

It is something you remember.

And once you remember it– nothing in your life stays the same.

## The Journey You're About to Take

This book is not meant to be rushed.
It's meant to be felt.

You are not here to fix yourself, improve yourself, or become someone else.
You are here to remember how to return to yourself
– gently, safely, and honestly.

Each chapter in this book builds on the one before it, guiding you through a process of awareness, regulation, and self-trust. You don't need to read it perfectly. You don't need to complete every exercise. You don't need to understand everything all at once.

Move at the pace your body trusts.

# Here's how this journey unfolds:

## Activation & Coherence

You'll begin by learning what coherence feels life
–the state where your heart and mind work together. This section
teaches you how to enter calm, grounded awareness and how to
return there when life pulls you away.

## Understanding Your Nervous System

You'll learn why you react the way you do, why emotions can feel
overwhelming, and why nothing about you is broken. This is where
self-blame softens and understanding begins.

## Intuition & Inner Knowing

As coherence strengthens, intuition becomes clearer. This part of the
journey helps you recognize the difference between fear and inner
guidance – and begin trusting what your body and heart already
know.

## Decision-Making & Alignment

You'll learn how to make choices from clarity instead of pressure, and how aligned decisions feel in the body. This is where self-trust becomes practical.

## Triggers, Anxiety, & Emotional Regulation

This section teaches you how to stay grounded when emotions rise, thoughts race, or anxiety appears. You'll learn how to feel without collapsing – and how to return to yourself without shame.

### Self-Worth, Belonging & Boundaries

Here, the journey turns inward. You'll begin rebuilding self-worth, learning how to protect your energy, and understanding which relationships support your coherence – and which ones don't.

## Relationships & Authentic Identity

You'll explore who you are around others, how authenticity feels in the body, and how to show up as yourself without shrinking or performing.

## Emotional Expression & Creativity

This part of the journey invites expression as healing. You'll learn how creativity, movement, writing, and art allow emotions and experiences to integrate safely – without needing words or explanations.

## The Body Remembers

You'll discover how the body holds experience, why certain reactions linger, and how healing happens gently through awareness, safety, and coherence – not force or reliving.

## Purpose & Meaning

The journey comes full circle as meaning emerges. You'll begin to see how your experiences shaped you, why your sensitivity matters, and how purpose unfolds naturally when you live in alignment.

This book doesn't give you answers from the outside. It helps you remember what you already carry within.

There is no finish line here.

Only returning.

Again and again.

# FIRST CHAPTER– ACTIVATION

*The Intelligence You Forgot You Had*

Most people think their power lives in their mind. That the brain is the command center, the decision maker, the source of everything they know.

But the truth is this:

Your brain was never meant to lead. It was meant to follow.

The strongest, most consistent signal in your body does not come from your brain at all. It comes from your heart.

Science has proven that the heart sends more information to the brain than the brain sends back. But long before studies existed, ancient cultures already understood this:
They knew the heart was not just an organ– it was intelligence.

If you've ever felt a knowing in your chest, a pull toward something you can't explain, a warning that protected you, or a truth you felt before you could speak it...

You've already accessed it.

Coherence is the state where this intelligence becomes available again.

It is the moment your body shifts out of survival and into clarity.
The moment your intuition becomes louder than your fear.
The moment your mind stops working against you and starts working with you.

And here is the secret no one ever taught you:

Coherence is not created. It is revealed.

It has always been there– beneath the stress, beneath the overthinking, beneath the noise of the world telling you who to be.

In this chapter, I'm going to teach you what coherence feels like, how to enter it, and how to use it to transform your life from the inside out.

But before we begin, I want you to understand something:

You are not broken.

You are not behind.

You are not missing anything.

Your heart already knows the way.

You are simply learning how to hear it again.

## What Coherence Feels Like

Coherence feels like coming home to yourself.

Your breathing softens.

Your shoulders drop.

Your mind becomes clearer, quieter, less frantic.

You stop trying to analyze what you feel.

You stop fighting yourself.

You shift.

And in that shift, something incredible happens:

Your heart and your brain begin to move in the same direction.

Your thoughts stop contradicting your feelings.

Your emotions stop pulling you backward.

Your nervous system stops hijacking your decisions.

This is why coherence feels like:

- calm without being numb
- clarity without overthinking
- confidence without forcing
- intuition without confusion
- groundedness without shutting down

Coherence is alignment of your inner world.

When you're in this state, life stops feeling like a battle.

You are no longer dragged by the mind or drowned by emotion.

You become steady– not perfect, but present.

And presence is where your power lives.

# Why You Lose Coherence

No one loses coherence because something is "wrong" with them.
You lose coherence because you were never taught how to keep it.

The world pulls you out of it constantly:

Stress

Fear

Noise

Comparison

Old trauma

Unprocessed emotions

Childhood conditioning

Your own thoughts looping on repeat

The nervous system goes into survival mode, the brain starts scanning for danger, and the heart's signal becomes chaotic and irregular.

When this happens:
- Your mind gets louder
- Your intuition gets quieter
- You emotions get heavier

- Your decisions get foggier
- Your body gets tense
- Your sleep becomes disrupted
- Your creativity shuts off

You don't shut down because you're weak– you shut down because your system is overwhelmed.

Coherence is the antidote.

## Entering Coherence: The First Shift

You do not enter coherence with force.

You enter it with permission.

Coherence begins with one simple truth:
Your body wants to feel safe.

When your body feels safe, your heart rhythm becomes smooth and organized, which sends a signal to your brain that life is no longer a threat.

This one shift unlocks:

- clearer thinking
- emotional regulation
- better decision-making
- stronger intuition
- healthier boundaries
- increased creativity

To activate this shift, we begin with the most powerful tool you have:

Your breath.

Not the breath you take when you're stressed– the breath you take when you remember yourself.

Let's begin.

## The Coherence Breath

This is your first activation.

1. Place your focus on your heart area. Imagine your attention moving from your head to your chest.

2. Slow your breathing. Inhale for 5 seconds. Exhale for 5 seconds. (coherent breathing always has equal inhale and exhale.)

3. Bring up a real, genuine emotion. Not something forced—something true:
   - gratitude
   - compassion
   - appreciation
   - love
   - relief
   - connection

4. Let your breath and your emotion move together. Imagine your heart glowing or expanding with each breath.

This is coherence.

Not the full state—but your gateway into it.
If you practice this for even 60 seconds, something in your body already shifted.
Your nervous system softened.
Your fear dialed down.

Your clarity turned up.

Your emotional charge lowered.

You just activated the energy of the heart– the intelligence you forgot you had.

## How Coherence Transforms Your Life From the Inside Out

Once you begin practicing coherence regularly, your life starts to reorganize itself around your new frequency.

Here's what changes:

### Your Relationships

You stop reacting from past wounds and start responding from clarity.

You communicate better.

You attract healthier people.

You see red flags more quickly.

**Your Emotions**

You stop drowning in them.

You stop avoiding them.

You learn to feel without collapsing.

Your anxiety lowers because you're no longer stuck in survival mode.

**Your Decision-Making**

Your choices become intuitive, aligned, and efficient.

You no longer choose out of fear or pressure.

You no longer betray yourself.

**Your identity**

You start to remember who you were before the world told you who to be.

Old stories fall away.

New possibilities open.

Your confidence becomes real– not forced.

**Your Future**

When your heart and brain are aligned,

Your actions shift,

Your emotions shift,

Your energy shifts,

And your entire timeline shifts.

Coherence doesn't just change how you feel.

It changes what becomes possible.

**The Activation is Complete**

You have just opened a doorway– one that many people never realize

exists.

You have felt your heart.

You have quieted your mind.

You have shifted your inner field.

You have begun the remembering.

The rest of this book will teach you:
- how to deepen that state
- how to recognize when you slip out of it
- how to regulate your emotions

- how to awaken intuition
- how to align your identity
- how to use coherence to create the life your heart has been trying to lead you toward

But for now, know this:

You are not learning coherence.
You are returning to it.

And your return changes everything.

# END OF CHAPTER ONE –ACTIVATION EXERCISES

*The Coherence Practice*

These exercises are simple on purpose. Coherence is not complicated– it is consistent.

Complete each one gently.

No pressure. No perfection.

Just presence.

## Exercise 1: The heart Drop-In (Two Minutes)

This is your daily starter practice.

1. Sit comfortably
2. Bring your attention from your head down into the center of your chest
3. Breathe in for 5 seconds, breathe out for 5 seconds.
4. Bring up a real emotion– not forced. Something small is enough:
   - the comfort of your bed

- appreciation for a person
- gratitude for a moment
- relief

5. Continue for 60-120 seconds

Notice what shifted.

Your breath? Your shoulders? Your thoughts?

This is coherence beginning.

## Exercise 2: The Mind Interrupt (Awareness)

Throughout the day, catch your mind in the act of:

- Spiraling
- Catastrophizing
- Looping on what-ifs
- Replaying the past
- Worrying about things you cannot control

When you catch it, pause and simply say:

**"This is a survival thought, not my truth."**

This statement interrupts the brain's fear pattern and signals your nervous system that you are safe.

Then breathe once into your heart.

You just shifted your state.

Exercise 3: The Coherence Scan

At the end of the day, ask yourself:

**"Was I in coherence today?"**

Rate your overall state from 1-10:
- 1-3 = out of coherence (survival mode)
- 4-6 = partial coherence (trying, shifting, stabilizing)
- 7-10 = (aligned, present, grounded)

This builds self-awareness and trains your body to recognize your inner signals.

## Reflection Questions

Write these in a journal or notes app– slowly.

1. Where in my life do I feel the most out of alignment with myself? (Your heart knows.)
2. What situations, people, or thoughts pull me out of coherence the most?
3. When I practiced the coherence breath, what shifted in my body? (Be specific. The more awareness you build, the stronger your coherence becomes.)
4. When was the last time I listened to my intuition and it was right? (This rebuilds trust)
5. What version of myself do I sense is trying to emerge?

## End-of-Chapter Intention

Read or whisper:

**"I allow my heart and mind to work together. I am safe to return to myself."**

# CHAPTER TWO

*The Science of Alignment: How Your Body Creates Coherence*

You have already felt coherence.

Even if only for a moment.
Even if subtly.

And now the mind wants to understand what just happened.

That is natural.

The brain seeks explanation.
The heart seeks truth.
Coherence is where they finally meet.

# Your Nervous System: The Hidden Architect of Your Life

Everything you experience– your mood, your reactions, your clarity, your creativity– is influenced by one powerful system often misunderstood:

Your nervous system.

It governs:

- whether you feel safe or threatened
- whether you feel calm or anxious
- whether you feel open or guarded
- whether you can access intuition or only fear

When your nervous system believes you are in danger, it activates survival mode.
This is not weakness.
This is biology.

But survival mode cannot create clarity.
It can only create protection.

Coherence happens when your nervous system receives a new message:

**You are safe.**

And when that message is received, everything changes.

## The Heart-Brain Conversation

The heart and brain are in constant communication through:

- the vagus nerve
- electromagnetic fields
- hormonal signals
- neural pathways

But here is what most people don't know:

The heart is not just a receiver
It is a sender

It sends rhythmic patterns of information to the brain that influence:

- emotional processing

- decision-making
- memory formation
- perception
- stress response

When you are anxious, overwhelmed, or emotionally charged, the heart's signal becomes irregular and chaotic. The brain interprets this as danger and responds with more fear, more tension, more reactivity.

This creates a loop.

But when the heart becomes steady and rhythmic, the brain shifts into clarity and higher reasoning.

This is coherence.

It is not mystical fantasy.
It is measurable, observable, and real.

Yet what science measures, the soul has always known.

## Incoherence vs Coherence

Let's make this simple.

Incoherence feels like

- overreacting
- mental fog
- emotional overwhelm
- racing thoughts
- insomnia
- tension
- confusion
- impulsivity
- exhaustion

Coherence feels like:

- calm
- clarity
- groundedness
- balanced emotion
- steady focus
- openness
- creativity

- intuitive knowing

One state shrinks your world.

The other expands it.

And the shift between them is not personality– it is physiology.

## Why Coherence Changes Your Reality

When you shift into coherence, your brain chemistry changes.
- cortisol decreases
- DHEA increases
- serotonin and dopamine balance
- the immune system strengthens
- cognitive function sharpens
- emotional regulation deepens

Your perception literally alters.

You see more clearly.

You respond instead of reacting

You access insight instead of panic.

This is why coherence doesn't just change how you feel– it changes how you interpret your world.

And your interpretation shapes your choices.

Your choices shape your future.

## The Role of Emotion in Coherence

Emotion is not the enemy of coherence.
Suppressed emotion is.

When you allow yourself to feel without judgment, coherence becomes accessible. When you fight emotion, the nervous system tightens, and clarity collapses.

The key is not to avoid feeling.
The key is to regulate feeling.
To hold it gently.
To breathe through it.
To allow it movement.

(**E**MOTION= Energy +Motion)

This is emotional intelligence.
This is coherence in action.


## The Moment You Shift

There is a sign you have entered coherence.

It may feel quiet.
Subtle.
Like still water instead of waves.

You stop needing to explain yourself.
You stop forcing understanding.
You stop asking "why" and start sensing "what now"
This is intelligence of alignment.

This is the body remembering how to lead.

# A New Relationship With Your Mind

Your mind is not the villain.

It was simply never meant to control the whole system.

In coherence, the mind changes its role.

Instead of:

- critic
- controller
- analyzer
- protector

It becomes

- translator
- observer
- supporter
- co-creator

The mind becomes a beautiful tool, not a prison.

And for many people, this is the moment their identity begins to shift.

## You Are Learning a New Language

The deeper you move into coherence, the more fluent you become in a new internal language:

The language of sensation
The language of intuition
The language of clarity
The language of stillness
The language of knowing

This language has always been yours.

You are not becoming something new.
You are learning to listen to something ancient.

## Preparation for What Comes Next

In the next chapter, you will learn how to recognize when you fall out of coherence– and how to guide yourself back without shame, force, or self-judgement.

Because the goal is not perfection.

The goal is awareness.

And awareness is the gateway to transformation.

Bring your attention to your chest for a final moment.

In hale slowly.

Exhale slowly.

Feel your breath soften.

There is nothing to fix.

Nothing to chase.

Only a rhythm to remember.

And it has always been yours.

# END OF CHAPTER TWO —EXERCISES

*Stabilising the Science in Your Body*

Chapter two explained what coherence is happening inside you. Now these exercises help you recognize it, build it, and gently train your system to return to it.

## Exercise 1: Safe Signal Breath

This practice teaches your body how to tell itself: **"I am okay."**

1. Sit or stand comfortably.
2. Place one hand on your chest.
3. Inhale slowly for 5 seconds.
4. Exhale slowly for 5 seconds.
5. As you breathe, silently say:
    - Inhale: *I am safe.*
    - Exhale: *I am here.*

Do this for 2-3 minutes

This rewires your nervous system to associate your breath with safety and calm.

## Exercise 2: The State Check-In

Once a day, pause and ask yourself:

- **Am I in survival mode right now?**
- **Or am I in clarity?**

Notice your body's answer before your mind explains it.

Signs you may be out of coherence:

- fast heartbeat
- irritation
- restless thoughts
- tension
- emotional numbness

No judgement. Just awareness.

Then take 3 coherent breaths and notice the shift.

## Exercise 3: The Emotional Translator

When you feel overwhelmed, stop and complete this sentence:

**"I feel _____ and my body is trying to protect me."**

Then place your hand on your heart and whisper:

**"Thank you for trying to keep me safe."**

This turns emotional chaos into understanding.

Understanding creates coherence.

## Exercise 4 (Mini Version): Color Awareness

Without drawing yet, simply notice:

**"What color feels like my emotional state today?"**

Write it down.

That's your emotional frequency speaking.

You're learning to listen to it.

## Reflection Questions (Chapter Two)

Journal gently:

1. When do I notice myself most out of coherence during the day?
2. What usually pulls me into survival mode?
3. Where in my body do I feel stress first?
4. When I slowed my breath, what changed?
5. What does 'feeling safe' actually mean for me?

## End-of-Chapter Intention

**"I honour the way my body protects me.**

**I choose awareness over judgment.**

**I return to balance."**

Now we move into the emotional heart of the journey.

# CHAPTER THREE

*When you Fall Out of Coherence (And How to Return Without Shame)*

Let's be clear about something important.

You will fall out of coherence.

You will overthink.

You will react.

You will feel overwhelmed.

You will feel anxious again.

This does not mean you are failing.

It means you are human.

Coherence is not a permanent state.

It is a rhythm.

A dance.

A practice of returning.

And the way you treat yourself when you fall out of alignment determines how quickly you come back.

## The Myth of "Always Calm"

Many people believe coherence means being calm all the time.

It doesn't.

It means becoming aware when you are not.

It means noticing instead of suppressing.
It means responding instead of shaming.
It means returning instead of judging.

Most people stay stuck because they criticize themselves for feeling too much.

Shame strengthens incoherence.

Compassion dissolves it.

## How You Know You've Slipped Out

You might notice:

- you're snapping at people
- your thoughts won't stop
- everything feels overwhelming
- your body feels tense or heavy
- you're replaying a moment again and again
- you're emotionally exhausted
- you feel disconnected from yourself

These are not failures.

These are signals.

Your body is saying:

**"I need safety. I need grounding. I need you."**

## The Return Is Gentle

The biggest mistake people make is trying to force calm.

Forcing creates more tension.

Tension creates more incoherence.

The return to coherence is soft.

It sounds like:

- "It's okay that I feel this."
- "I'm allowed to pause."
- "This moment will not last forever."
- "I can breathe again."

The moment you stop fighting yourself, your nervous system listens.

## The 3-Step Return Process

When you noticed you've slipped out, follow this:

1. Name it

**"I am overwhelmed right now."**
Naming creates distance from the emotion.

2. Breathe it

5 second inhale.
5 second exhale.
Three times.

3. Soften it

Place your hand on your heart and say:
**"I'm here with you."**

That's it.
No fixing. No solving. Just presence.

Presence restores coherence.

## What Teens Need to Hear (And What Adults Forgot)

You are not "too emotional."
You are not "dramatic."
You are not weak for feeling deeply.

You have a sensitive system because you were meant to feel life fully.

The goal is not to shut your emotions down.
The goal is to guide them safely.

Coherence teaches you how.

## Falling Out Is Part of Mastery

Everytime you fall out of coherence and guide yourself back, you build:

- emotional strength
- nervous system stability
- self-trust
- resilience
- intuitive clarity

You are not regressing.
You are strengthening the pathway home.

## A New Relationship With Yourself

When you stop shaming your emotions, you unlock leadership over your inner world.

Instead of saying:
"What's wrong with me?"

You begin asking:
"What is my body trying to show me?"

This is the foundation of emotional intelligence.

This is where real growth begins.

## A Final Reminder

You do not rise because you never fall.
You rise because you learn how to return.

And every return makes your coherence stronger.

# END OF CHAPTER THREE

# –EXERCISES

*Learning the Return*

Chapter Three teaches the truth:

Falling out of coherence is normal.

Returning is the skill.

These exercises help strengthen that return.

## Exercise 1: The "I Noticed" Pause

When you feel overwhelmed, irritated, or mentally flooded, stop and say:

**"I noticed...."**

Examples:

- "I noticed I'm getting tense."
- "I noticed my thoughts are racing."
- "I noticed my heart is beating fast."

This does two powerful things:

1. It stops the emotional spiral.
2. It puts you back in the observer role instead of the panic role.

Then take one slow inhale and exhale.

Just one.
That's the doorway.


## Exercise 2: Hand-to-Heart Grounding

Place your palm gently on your chest.

Whisper (out loud or in your mind):

**"I'm here."**
**"You're okay."**
**"We can slow down."**

This sends a direct neurological signal of safety to your brain.

Your body listens to your tone more than your thoughts.

## Exercise 3:  Three-Count Reset

This is your quick coherence recovery tool.

1. Inhale for 3 seconds.
2. Exhale for 3 seconds.
3. Repeat 3 times.

This resets your heart rhythm and stops the physiological stress response.

It's small on purpose– teens especially need tools that don't feel overwhelming.

## Exercise 4: Emotion Labeling Without Judging

When you feel a big emotion, write or say:

**"Right now, I'm feeling _____".**
And it's okay to feel this."

Label it gently–

Not as a problem, but as an experience.

This builds emotional intelligence and takes the "danger" out of the feeling.

## Exercise 5: The 60- Second Return

Set a timer for one minute.

During that minute:
- Breathe slowly
- Soften your shoulders
- Place one hand on your chest
- Imagine your breath moving into and out of your heart

Focus only on the sensation of your heart area.

When the timer goes off, notice how different you feel.

One minute can change an entire day.

## Reflection Questions (Chapter Three)

These journal prompts help you understand your emotional patterns:

1. What emotion pulls me out of coherence the fastest?

2. What do I normally tell myself when I'm overwhelmed?

3. What could I tell myself instead?

4. What does "shame-free returning" look like for me?

5. When was the last time I returned to calm without anyone guiding me?

These questions build self-awareness + self-compassion – the foundation of coherence.

## End-of-Chapter Intention

**"I don't judge myself for feeling.
I guide myself back with kindness.
Every return strengthens me."**

# CHAPTER FOUR

*Intuition & Inner Knowing: Hearing the Voice Beneath the Noise*

There is a version of you that already knows what to do.

Not from fear.

Not from Pressure.

Not from overthinking.

But from a quiet, steady truth that lives beneath everything else.

That truth is your intuition.

Intuition is not magic.

It is not guessing.

It is not some special gift that only certain people have.

It is a biological and energetic guidance system that every human is born with.

Most people lost access to it because life got too loud.

Your intuition didn't go away.

It got buried.

And in coherence, it rises again.

## What Intuition Actually is (The Science + The Soul)

Intuition is the way your heart communicates with you before your mind has time to analyze.

Science calls it:

- pattern recognition
- neuroception
- emotional memory
- somatic intelligence
- the brain-heart feedback loop

Spiritual traditions call it:

- inner knowing
- the higher self
- the soul's voice
- guidance remembering

Both are talking about the same thing:

Information that comes from within – before thought, before logic, before fear.

Intuition is fast.

Fear is loud.

Wisdom is quiet.

Trauma is reactive.

Your job is to learn the difference.

## How Intuition Speaks

Intuition rarely uses full sentences.

It uses signals.

It speaks through:

- a tightness in your chest
- a gentle pull toward something
- a sinking feeling when something's off
- the sudden urge to pause

- a thought that appears out of nowhere
- a picture in your mind
- a calm "yes"
- a heavy "no"
- goosebumps
- a sense of familiarity
- a feeling that someone or something isn't right

Teens especially feel intuition strongly – they just haven't learned to trust it yet.

Adults feel it too, but many have been trained to ignore it. Coherence restores the connection.

## The Problem Isn't That You Don't Know – It's That You Don't Trust

Most people can sense that truth but don't trust what they feel, because:

- they were taught to listen to authority over instinct.

- they were told "you're being dramatic" or "you're overreacting."
- their environment punished sensitivity.
- fear became louder than intuition.
- they learned to doubt themselves to stay safe.

But here's the real truth:

Your intuition never left.
You just learned to override it.

Chapter 4 is about reversing that.

## Intuition vs. Fear (The Key Difference)

You must learn this distinction – it will change your life:

Intuition is calm.
Even when it says "no."

Fear is urgent.
It rushes. It pushes. It panics.

Intuition gives direction.

Fear gives noise.

Intuition feels like clarity,

Fear feels like chaos.

Intuition is steady.

Fear is dramatic.

Intuition speaks once.

Fear repeats itself over and over.

If the feeling is chaotic, sharp, or panicky – it's fear.

If the feeling is quiet, grounded, or subtle – its intuition.

This one difference can save years of confusion.

## Why Intuition Becomes Louder in Coherence

When your heart and brain sync, your nervous system relaxes.

When your body feels safe, your inner signals come through more clearly.

When your mind stops spiraling, your intuition isn't drowned out.

Coherence creates the perfect environment for intuitive clarity.

Most people think intuition is random.

It's not.

It's predictable.

It's consistent.

It has patterns.

It strengthens with practice.

And your body is designed for it.

## The Small Whisper You Keep Ignoring

Every single day, your intuition sends you tiny signals:

- "Don't go there."
- "Reach out to that person."
- "Something feels off."

- "Say no."
- "Slow down."
- "This is the right path."

It's not loud because it doesn't need to yell.

Fear yells.

Trauma yells.

Wounds yell.

Intuition whispers.

Your coherence practice is training your ears to hear that whisper again.

## The Body Never Lies

This is one of the most powerful truths you will ever learn:

Your body feels the truth before your mind understands it.

If something feels wrong – it is.

If something feels off – it is.

If someone's energy tightens your chest – pay attention.

If a situation feels heavy – step back.

If a choice feels peaceful – move toward it.

Your body is speaking long before your thoughts start debating.

Learning to trust that signal is life-changing.

## Intuition Is Not Mystical
## —It's Remembered

Intuition is not about seeing the future.

It's about recognizing the truth in the present.

You don't need to develop intuition.

You need to remove the noise blocking it.

Coherence quiets the noise.

Awareness strengthens the signal.

Practice sharpens the clarity.

Trust completes the process.

## The Beginning of Self-Trust

You cannot build intuition without self-trust.

And you cannot build self-trust if you shame yourself for being wrong.

This chapter will teach you how to:

- listen
- trust
- recognize
- follow

Because intuition is a muscle –

And coherence is the gym.

## Your Inner Knowing Is Rising

By the end of this book, your intuition will not just be something you "feel."

It will be something you can use:

- to navigate relationships
- to make aligned decisions
- to protect your energy
- to choose healthy boundaries
- to avoid unnecessary pain
- to recognize opportunity
- to sense people clearly
- to understand your emotions
- to choose your path

Your intuition is not a myth.

It is a light you forgot how to turn on.

This chapter is your switch.

# END OF CHAPTER FOUR –EXERCISES

*Hearing the Voice Beneath the Noise*

These exercises help you learn how intuition speaks in your body, and how to follow it without fear or doubt.

## Exercise 1: Intuition vs. Fear Check

When you feel a strong reaction or decision moment, pause and ask:

Is this calm or chaotic?

Does this feel steady or panicked?

Write down what you notice:

Moment?

What I felt?

Calm or Chaotic?

Intuition or fear?

This trains the brain to recognize intuitive clarity vs. emotional noise.

## Exercise 2: The Coherence Question

Take three slow heart-focused breaths.

Then ask:

**"What does my heart want me to know right now?"**

Don't overthink.

Write the first sentence that comes through - even if it feels too simple.

Intuition always arrives before doubt.

## Exercise 3: Body Compass Scan

Your body already knows "yes" and "no."

Do this:

1. Think of something you love – a person, a place, a memory.
   Notice how your body feels.
   (This is your "yes" feeling.)

2. Think of something you dislike – a food, a situation, a place you avoid.

> Notice how your body feels.

> (This is your "no" feeling.)

Now you understand your body's language.

Use this anytime you're unsure.

## Exercise 4: First Answer Only

At least once today, make a small decision instantly:

- what to wear
- where to sit
- which route to take
- who to text back
- what to eat for a snack

Say:

**"First answer is the right answer."**

This teaches your brain to stop arguing with your heart.

## Exercise 5: Coincidence Journal

Write down:

- any moment that feels like "I just knew"
- anytime something worked out after a feeling told you so
- any "right place, right time" situation
- any person you thought of – then they texted or walked up
- any "red flag" you felt that turned out to be true

This creates evidence.

Evidence creates trust.

Trust strengthens intuition.

## Reflection Questions (Chapter Four)

Journal these slowly:

1. What does intuition feel like in my body?

2. When was the last time I ignored my intuition and regretted it?
3. When was the last time I trusted it and it was right?
4. What fears make me doubt myself?
5. What would change in my life if I trusted my inner knowing more often?

These questions deepen awareness – and self-trust.

## End-of-Chapter Intention

Read aloud or quietly...

**"My heart speaks with truth.**
**My mind learns to listen.**
**I trust the knowing that lives inside me."**

# CHAPTER FIVE

*Your Inner Compass*

*–Making Decisions from Alignment*

Everyday, you make choices.

Some are small:

- what to wear
- where to sit
- who to text back

Some are big:

- who you trust
- what you believe about yourself
- what direction your life is going

But here's what's wild:

Most people make decisions from fear instead of alignment.

Fear asks:

"What if something goes wrong?"

Alignment asks:

"What if this is right?"

Fear prevents.
Alignment guides.

This chapter teaches you how to choose from the place inside you that already knows who you're becoming.

## Every Choice Leads You Toward or Away from Your Future

Every decision you make – even the small ones – shifts your timeline.

You are either choosing:

- the future that expands you

    Or

- the future that restricts you

There is no neutral choice.

Even ignoring the decision is a decision.

Your life is created moment by moment by the direction you allow yourself to move.

## Why Decision-Making Is So Hard

Most people don't struggle with knowing what they want.

They struggle with:
- doubting what they want
- worrying what others will think
- overthinking what could go wrong
- avoiding discomfort
- trying to meet expectations
- choosing safety over authenticity

The fear of making the "wrong" choice keeps them from making the right one.

Staying stuck is still a choice –
And it often hurts more than moving forward.

## When You Are In Coherence,

Decisions Become Obvious

Because the heart and brain agree:
There is no tug-of-war.
There is no confusion.
There is no overthinking.

You feel the truth in your body.

Good decisions feel:

- steady
- peaceful
- grounded
- clean

Bad decisions feel:

- heavy
- rushed
- sticky
- anxious

Your body knows before your mind does.

## Three Types of Decisions

Every choice you make falls into one of these:

### 1. Aligned Decisions

These support your highest self.
You feel relief or excitement afterward.

Example:
Setting a healthy boundary, taking a positive risk.

### 2. Fear-Based Decisions

These protect the ego but limit the soul.

You feel anxious or regretful afterward.

Example:

Saying yes because you're scared to say no.

### 3. Avoidance Decisions

These delay discomfort but create bigger problems later.

Example:

Ignoring intuition about a friend or relationship.

The more coherent you become, the easier it is to choose alignment over fear.

## What "Alignment" Actually Means

Alignment is when your:

- intuition
- emotions

- body
- values
- future self

all point in the same direction.

Alignment feels like:

- "This is who I am."
- "This is where I'm meant to go."
- "This feels like relief."
- "This makes me feel proud of myself."

If a decision betrays your inner truth –
It's misaligned.

Stop Asking: "Is This Right?"

Start Asking:
**"Is this true?"**
**"Does this support who I'm becoming?"**
**"Does this move me forward or backward?"**

Your life changes when you switch the questions you ask.

## If You Aren't Sure, The Answer is "Not Yet."

Confusion is a sign to pause.

Not a sign to panic.

If you can't feel the intuitive "yes" or "no,"

You're not in coherence – yet.

Breathe.

Ground.

Come back.

Then decide.

Never rush a decision when your heart isn't online.

## The Most Powerful Words in Alignment

No

A full sentence.

A sacred boundary.

A shield for your future.

Yes

A doorway.

A leap.

A declaration that you are worthy of more.

You become unstoppable when you no protects your yes

## Your Intuition Wants to Lead You Somewhere

You are being guided to a version of yourself that already exists –
the one who is confident, clear, and aligned.

Decision-making is how you walk toward that version every single day.

Coherence keeps the path visible.

Your heart keeps the compass steady.

Your courage keeps your feet moving.

## You Already Know the Way

Every aligned life begins with a single choice:
trusting yourself more than you doubt yourself.

When you start making decisions from coherence instead of fear...
everything changes.

# END OF CHAPTER FIVE –EXERCISES

*Training Your Inner Compass*

These exercises help you practice choosing the direction your future self wants.

## Exercise 1: The 2-Questions Decision Test

Before any choice – big or small – pause and ask:

1. Does this feel like expansion or contraction?
   (Do I feel open or restricted)

2. Does this support who I'm becoming?
   (Or does this keep me who I was?)

If the answer is expansion + support → Yes

If the answer is contraction + fear → No

If mixed → Wait until coherent

This is your new decision filter.

## Exercise 2: The Body Compass

Place your hand over your heart.

Ask you body:

### "Which direction feels peaceful?"

Then notice:

- Heaviness = "Not this"
- Lightness = "Move here"
- Tightness = "Something's off"
- Excitement = "This is aligned!"

Your heart never lies.

## Exercise 3: The Pause Before React

The moment you feel pressure to decide quickly –

Stop.

Whisper:

**"If it required me to rush,
it's not in alignment."**

Then take 3 coherence breaths.

A wise decision never comes from panic.

## Exercise 4:  Evidence of Alignment

Write down 3 times in your life when you trusted your gut and it turned out right:

1.

2.

3.

Your brain needs reminders that intuition has a track record.

Trust grows with proof.

## Exercise 5: One Aligned Action Per Day

Every day choose 1 small thing from your heart:

- send the message
- take the walk
- say no
- say yes
- start the project
- stop the thing draining you
- listen to the nudge

Write it down to celebrate the shift:

Today's aligned action:_____

Alignment becomes a habit.

A habit becomes a lifestyle.

A lifestyle becomes a new timeline.

## Reflection Questions (Chapter Five)

Journal these slowly:

1.  When I think of who I want to become...
    What choices get me closer to that version?

2.  What choices usually lead me away from myself?

3.  What fear shows up most when I decide to choose differently?

4.  How would my life change if I trusted myself first?

5.  What would the bravest version of me choose today?

These questions turn decision-making into identity creation.

## End of Chapter Intention

Speak aloud to anchor it into your nervous system....

**"I choose from my future, not my fear. My heart leads, my mind supports, and every decision transforms me."**

# CHAPTER SIX

*Emotional Triggers*

*–Stay in Coherence When Life Happens*

It's easy to feel balanced when everything is calm. But real life isn't calm all the time.

A text message can change your whole mood.

Someone's tone can shake your confidence.

One comment can send you into a spiral.

Your emotions can flip from 0 to 100 instantly.

And here's the truth:

That doesn't mean you're weak.

It means you're human.

Your nervous system is constantly scanning for danger – even emotional danger.

A trigger is simply a signal that your body feels unsafe.

Coherence teaches you how to respond instead of react.

## What Is a Trigger? (Simple and True)

A trigger is anything that causes a sudden shift in your emotional state, usually because:

- it reminds your nervous system of a past hurt
- it threatens your identity
- it threatens your belonging
- it makes you feel judged, rejected, or powerless

It's not about the situation itself –
It's about what the situation means to your mind and body.

Example:

Someone ignores your message →

Your nervous system says:

"Are we being abandoned?"

Even if that's not the truth, your body feels like it is.

## Where Triggers Come From

Triggers are built from:

- old experiences
- past relationships
- moments of embarrassment or shame
- fear of not being good enough
- fear of being left out
- memories your mind forgot but your body didn't

The trigger isn't the enemy.
It is a map – pointing you to a place that still needs care.

## What Happens in Your Body During a Trigger

Your heart rhythm becomes chaotic

Your breath becomes shallow

Your muscles tighten

Your thoughts race

Your emotions spike

This is your body saying:

"Protect! Something hurts!"

It's the survival system activating –
Even when the danger is emotional, not physical.

Coherence helps your system realize:

"I am uncomfortable, but I am not unsafe."

That distinction changes everything.

## The Trigger Trap

Most people do one of these:

- ❖ React explosively

"Screw this. I'm done."
Yelling, shutting down, blocking people, isolating.

- ❖ Blame themselves

"What's wrong with me?"
Spiraling deeper into fear and shame.

Both reactions increase incoherence.
Both reactions make the trigger stronger next time.

There is another path:

Recognize. Regulate. Return.

## The Coherence Reset for Triggers

The moment you feel yourself slipping:

Step 1 – Name It

"I'm triggered right now."
(This separates YOU from the FEELING.)

Step 2 – Breathe It

3 slow breaths into the heart area.

(Even ONE breath changes your physiology.)

Step 3 – Normalize It

"It makes sense that this hurts."
(Shame dissolves. Safety increases.)

Now the trigger loses its power.

The body relaxes.

The mind clears.

You return to yourself.

## Triggers Are Teachers

Instead of asking:

"Why am I like this?"

Ask:

"What is this moment trying to heal?"

Every trigger reveals:

- a wound

- a belief
- a fear
- a story your holding
- a part of you asking for attention

Triggers are invitations to understand yourself more deeply.

## You Are Allowed to Feel the Full Emotion

Coherence does not mean being calm all the time.
It means knowing how to come home when emotion pulls you out.

Feel it fully.
Then guide yourself back gently.

That is emotional strength.
That is maturity.
That is power.

## Nothing Is Wrong With You

If you get triggered easily:

You are not broken.

You are not dramatic.

You are not "too sensitive."

It means your system is alert because you care.

Your sensitivity is not flaw –

It is a superpower that coherence teaches you to control.

## The Return Is the Win

Not the "never getting triggered."

Not the "being calm all the time."

The return.

The recovery.

The ability to say:

**"I felt that. It was a lot.**

**But I'm still here. And I know how to come back."**

This is coherence in the real world.

And it changes everything.

# END OF CHAPTER SIX —EXERCISES

*Regulating When You're Triggered*

These exercises help you return to coherence when emotions feel too big.

## Exercise 1: Name the Trigger, Don't Be the Trigger

When you feel your mood shift suddenly, pause and say:

**"I am feeling triggered – this is a reaction, not a reality."**

Then write:

- What happened?
- What emotion rushed in?
- What story did my mind instantly create?

Awareness disarms the trigger's power.

## Exercise 2: The 10-second Rescue

Do this anywhere. Even in public.

- Inhale for 5 seconds
- Exhale for 5 seconds
- Repeat twice
- Hand on heart if possible

This interrupts the stress signal and resets your nervous system quickly.

If you can breathe... you can return.

## Exercise 3: Reassure the Body

Whisper or think:

"This feels intense,
but I am safe."

This tells your body the truth

–and replaces panic with presence.

## Exercise 4: The Filter Check

Ask yourself:

**"Did I react to what happened –
or to what I believed it meant?"**

Most triggers come from interpretation, not reality.

Write down the fact vs. the story:

- The Fact – _____

- The story I told myself – _____

Understanding this difference is healing.

## Exercise 5: Replace Self-Judgment With Care

Fill in the blanks:

**"It makes sense that I felt _____,
because _____happened."**

This creates compassion – not shame.

Compassion brings you back to coherence faster than force ever will.

## Bonus: The "Walk Away, Come Back" Strategy

When the trigger is too hot to handle:

1. Step away.
2. Breathe.
3. Return when your heart feels steady.

Taking space is strength – not avoidance.

## Reflection Questions (Chapter Six)

Journal these slowly after your body has calmed:

1.  What situation triggered me the most this week and why?
2.  What emotion usually shows up first when I'm triggered?
3.  What does that emotion need – support, protection, or expression?
4.  How quickly did I return to coherence this time compared to before?
5.  What did I learn about myself through this trigger?

Triggers become teachers when you learn their language.


### End-of-Chapter Intention

Say this gently to your heart...

**"My emotions are valid.**
**My reactions are human.**
**My return is powerful."**

# CHAPTER SEVEN

*Anxiety*

*—When Your Mind Won't Get Quiet*

Anxiety is one of the hardest internal battles a person can face – especially when no one else can see it.

People may look calm on the outside while inside they feel:

- a fast heart
- a tight chest
- a storm of thoughts
- a feeling of "something is wrong"

And sometimes... you can't even explain why.

That's the thing about anxiety:

It doesn't need a reason to show up.
The nervous system believes there might be danger –
So it sounds the alarm just in case.

Your body tries to protect you.

But it doesn't always get the message right.

## What Anxiety Actually Is

Anxiety is not just worry.

It is your body preparing for a threat that doesn't exist.

The survival system turns on:

- adrenaline increases
- heart rate rises
- breathing speeds up
- muscles tense
- thoughts become focused on danger

Your brain tries to solve a problem that isn't real.

So the mind starts inventing one.

That's why anxiety feels like:
- "What if I can't handle this?
- "What if they're judging me?"

- "What if I mess up?"
- "What if something bad happens?"

The most exhausting part is not the anxiety itself –
it's arguing with your thoughts trying to stop it.


## What Anxiety Isn't

Anxiety is NOT:

- weakness
- attention seeking
- immaturity
- overreacting
- "being dramatic"

Anxiety is a nervous system response – not a personality trait.

You are not anxious.
You are experiencing anxiety.

There is a difference.

## How Anxiety Disconnects You from Coherence

Anxiety tries to take control of your body by:

- speeding up breath
- tightening the chest
- sending chaotic signals from heart to brain

Your mind then spirals trying to make sense of the chaos:
"What's wrong with me? Why can't I stop?"

This creates a loop:

Body alerts brain → Brain panics → Body intensifies alert → repeat

When the mind get loud,
The heart gets quiet –
and coherence disappears.

This chapter is about reversing that.

## Anxiety Isn't Random
## —It Has Patterns

Anxiety appears most when you feel:

- watched
- judged
- trapped
- unprepared
- out of control
- responsible for too much
- not good enough
- like something is about to go wrong

These aren't personality flaws.

They are threats to belonging, identity, or safety.

Your nervous system protects what matters most to you.

## Anxiety is Loud – Intuition is Quiet

Anxiety yells:

"Fix it now! Something bad will happen!"

Intuition whispers:

"You are safe. Breathe."

Anxiety forces urgency.
Intuition offers clarity.

If it's loud, chaotic, and repetitive –
it's fear, **not** inner knowing.

This simple truth can save years of confusion.

## You Don't Have to Fight Anxiety

Most people try to defeat anxiety by:

- distracting
- suppressing
- escaping
- Pretending they're okay

But what you fight gets stronger.

Coherence teaches a different approach:

You don't fight anxiety.
You guide your body out of survival mode.

You show your nervous system:
"We're not in danger anymore."

Relief begins the moment your body believes you again.

## There's Nothing Wrong With You

If you experience anxiety often:

You are not failing.

You are not falling apart.

Your system is not broken.

It is doing its job –

Just at the wrong times and with too much intensity.

You're not weak.

You're overwhelmed.

And overwhelm can be healed.

## The Goal Isn't to Eliminate Anxiety

The goal is to:
- recognize it early
- regulate it quickly
- prevent the spiral
- trust yourself again

Just like falling out of coherence,

anxiety is not the problem –

staying stuck in it is.

And you're learning how to shift.

## You Can Take Your Power Back

By the end of this chapter and the next exercises, you will be able to:

- restore safety in your nervous system
- calm racing thoughts
- stop spirals before they take over
- breathe again when everything feels tight
- find stability inside chaos

Anxiety doesn't get the final word.

You do.

Because the part of you that leads – *your heart* –
Has been waiting to take the wheel back.

And it's ready now.

# END OF CHAPTER SEVEN –EXERCISES

Taking Back Control When Your Mind Gets Loud

These are not distractions.

These are nervous system reset tools that work quickly and anywhere.

## Exercise 1: The Coherent Calm Breath

Use this the moment anxiety hits.

1. Inhale through your nose for 4 seconds
2. Exhale through your mouth for 6 seconds
3. Place your hand over your heart
4. Repeat for 60-90 seconds

Why it works:

A longer exhale tells your brain "the danger is gone" and shuts off the panic response.

You are sending safety signals to your body.

## Exercise 2: Name the Experience, Reduce the Power

Say out loud or in your mind:

**"My body is trying to protect me.
This is a feeling, not a fact."**

Then label what's happening:

- My heart is beating fast."
- "My thoughts are racing."
- "I feel sacred."

When you name it → you take control back from it.

## Exercise 3: The Reality Check

Ask yourself these three grounding questions:

1. What is happening *right now*, this exact moment?

2. What is the most likely reality?

3. What is within my control in the next 2 minutes?

Anxiety shrinks when truth gets bigger.

## Exercise 4: The 5–4–3–2–1 Reset

Use this if you feel like you're spiraling:

- 5 things you can see

- 4 things you can touch

- 3 things you can hear

- 2 things you can smell

- 1 thing you can taste (or imagine tasting)

This brings you out of your thoughts and back into your body.

Your nervous system relaxes when you return to the present moment.

## Exercise 5: The Loop Breaker Phrase

Say this firmly:

**"I am not my thoughts.**
**I am the one noticing them."**

This instantly shifts you out of the emotional storm and into the observer role
– which is coherence.

## Reflection Questions (Chapter Seven)

Journal these after the anxiety releases:

1. What usually triggers my anxiety the most?
2. What is the first sign my body gives me when anxiety shows up?
3. What calming strategy worked best for me today?
4. What did my anxiety try to protect me from?
5. What truth was uncovered after the panic calmed?

Anxiety becomes a teacher when fear becomes information.

## End-Of-Chapter Intention

Place your hand over your heart + breathe...

**"I am safe to slow down.**
**My thoughts are not danger.**
**Calm is my new power."**

# CHAPTER EIGHT

*Self-Worth & Belonging*

*–Remembering Who You Really Are*

Every human has the same deepest questions:

"Am I enough?"

"Am I wanted?"

"Do I matter?"

Anxiety makes you doubt it.

Triggers make you forget it.

Past experiences convince you of lies:

- "I'm too much"
- "I'm not enough"
- "People always leave"
- "I don't fit anywhere"
- "I'm replaceable"
- "I have to earn love"

These beliefs don't show up as thoughts first –

They show up as shame, fear, and shrinking.

Your nervous system tells you a story about your worth long before your brain does.

And it's time to rewrite that story.


## Self-Worth is Not a Personality Trait

It is not something you earn.
It is not something you prove.
It is not decided by grades, achievements, looks, or popularity.

Self-worth is your birthright.

You were enough the moment you existed.

The world didn't teach you that –
But it's the truth your heart always knew.

# Where Worthiness Gets Damaged

Self-worth cracks when:

- someone you care about pulled away
- you were compared to others
- you felt invisible
- you were bullied or laughed at
- you felt like you weren't chosen
- you were told to be different to be loved
- you tried your best and it still wasn't enough for someone

Your brain recorded those moments.

Your nervous system believed them.

Your identity adapted to survive them.

But that adaptation was protection – not truth.

# Belonging Is Not About Fitting In

Fitting in says:

"Change to be accepted"

Belonging says:

"Be yourself and feel safe doing it."

Fitting in is performance.
Belonging is connection.

Fitting in exhausts you.
Belonging nourishes you.

Coherence guides you back to belonging –
starting with belonging to yourself.

## Your Brain Has Been Protecting You From Rejection

When you walk into a room and feel overwhelmed by thoughts like:

- "Everyone is judging me"
- "I don't know what to say"
- "They're all better than me"

- "I shouldn't be here"

That is not insecurity –
that is ancient survival wiring.

Rejection used to mean danger.
Being left out used to mean death for humans in tribes.

So your nervous system still reacts like:
"Belonging = survival."

This isn't weakness.
This is biology.

And you can change the signal.

## Coherence Rebuilds Worth

When your heart and mind sync, you feel:

- grounded in who you are
- confident without forcing it

- calm in your own skin
- less afraid of judgement
- less likely to shrink yourself

Self-worth is not found in accomplishments.

It is restored by remembering:
**"I am already enough."**

Coherence lets you feel that truth in your body –
Not just hear it in a quote.

## You Don't Have to Earn Space

You deserve to take up space.
You deserve to exist exactly as you are.
You deserve to breathe without apologizing.
You deserve to feel seen, safe, and valued.

Your worth is not up for debate.
Not even with yourself.

## You Are Not "Too Sensitive"
## –You Are Highly Aware

The world has taught sensitive people to feel ashamed of their depth.
But sensitivity is data, empathy, and intuition.

It's your ability to read energy.
It's your heart speaking loudly.
It's your superpower – not a flaw.

Your sensitivity is what makes you capable of connection.

The world needs people who feel this much.

## Belonging Begins With Self-Belonging

The more you try to be what others want,
the more disconnected you become with yourself.

When you start choosing what feels true inside your heart –
the right people will feel like home to you.

Your coherence attracts coherence.

That's how real belonging happens.

## Your Self-Worth Is Coming Home

All the places inside you that feel unloved are opening again.
All the moments you felt rejected or ignored are being rewritten.

Every exercise you've done so far has prepared you for this chapter.

Your heart remembers your worth even when your mind forgets.

You are not becoming enough.
You are remembering that you always were.

# END OF CHAPTER EIGHT –EXERCISES

*Rebuilding Self-Worth & Belonging*

These practices help you reconnect with yourself – and feel like you belong in your own life.

## Exercise 1: Mirror Truth

Stand in front of a mirror.

Look into your own eyes (not your hair, not your skin – your eyes).

Say:

**"I deserve to take up space."**
**"I am allowed to be exactly who I am."**

Even if you feel awkward – that's okay.

Your nervous system is hearing a new truth.

## Exercise 2: The "Thank You" Shift

When you mess up or feel embarrassed, instead of saying:

- "I'm so stupid"
- "Why am I like this?"
- "I always ruin things"

Place your hand over your chest and whisper:

**"Thank you, body, for trying to protect me."**
**"I'm learning. I'm growing."**

Self-compassion rewires shame.

## Exercise 3: Belonging Inventory

Write down 5 places or moments when you felt safe being yourself:

1.
2.
3.

4.

5.

These are your belonging environments.

Spend more time there.

Spend less time where you shrink.

## Exercise 4: Identity Alignment

Finish these sentences:

- I feel most like myself when I....
- People who make me feel seen do this...
- I love when I show this part of me...

These answers reveal who you truly are –

not who you learned to be.

Follow that feeling.

## Exercise 5: Replace the Lie

Write down one core belief you've been holding that hurts you:

Example:

"I'm not good enough."

"I bother people."

"No one really cares about me."

Then rewrite it as your heart knows it:

**"I am more than enough."**

**"I am loved and valued."**

**"I deserve connection."**

Say the new belief every day – even before you believe it.

Your brain will adjust to your heart's truth.

# Reflection Questions (Chapter Eight)

Journal these at night or in a calm moment:

1. Whose voice first made me question my worth
   – and do I still want that voice influencing me?

2. When do I feel most proud of who I am?

3. Who supports the real me – not the edited version?

4. What parts of myself have I been hiding, and why?

5. If I loved myself fully, what would I stop apologizing for?

These questions are identity therapy.

## End-of-Chapter Intention

say this with your hand over your heart...

**"I belong here.**

**My worth is not earned – it is remembered.**

**I choose myself now."**

# CHAPTER NINE

*Boundaries & Energy Protection*

*–Keeping You Coherence Safe*


You can do all the inner work in the world...

But if your environment drains you or disrespects you –

Staying in coherence becomes exhausting.


Boundaries are not walls.

They are filters:


What energy gets in.

What energy stays out.

What energy you allow to influence your nervous system.


Your peace is precious – and it deserves protection.


## Why Boundaries Are Required (Not Optional)


Healthy boundaries say:

- "This is what I allow."
- "This is what I deserve."
- "This is what I won't carry anymore."
- "This is how you can treat me."
- "This is how I will treat myself."

Boundaries are not about controlling others.
They are about choosing yourself.

Every yes without boundaries...
is a silent no to your own well-being.

## How Energy Impacts Coherence

Some people regulate you:
You feel calmer, safer, lighter around them

Others dysregulate you:
Your heart rate shifts, chest tightens, thoughts race.

Your nervous system is constantly reading energy.

Trust it.

It knows who is good for your heart and who only activates your fear.

## The Signals Your Body Sends

When someone is crossing your boundary or draining you, your body will tell you:

- sudden anxiety
- feeling small
- tight throat or chest
- urge to disappear
- guilt for feeling upset
- replaying what happened
- feeling "off" after hanging out with them

These are not random feelings.
These are messages.

Your body is saying:
"This energy doesn't feel safe."

## Why Setting Boundaries Feels Scary

Because many people grew up learning:

- "Don't make others uncomfortable."
- "Be easygoing."
- "Don't cause conflict."
- "Be nice no matter what."
- "Your needs can wait."
- "Don't upset anyone."

That teaches your nervous system:

"Other people's comfort is more important than mine."

Boundaries shift that belief to:

"Respect goes both ways."

## Boundaries Are Acts of Self-Respect

When you set a boundary, you're saying:

**"I believe I am worthy of protection."**

That is self-worth in action.

That is coherence in relationships.

Boundaries are not mean.

Boundaries are clarity.


## Three Levels of Boundaries

Boundaries can be:


### 1. Internal

How you speak to yourself

How you treat yourself

What thoughts you allow to take root

Example:

"I won't talk to myself like I'm the problem."


### 2. Interpersonal

How others can treat you

What behaviors you accept

What dynamics you refuse


Example:

"I am not okay with being yelled at or mocked."


### 3.  Environmental


Where you go

Who you spend time with

What situations you avoid to protect your peace


Example:

"I don't have to stay where I feel unsafe or unseen."


## Boundaries and Love Can Coexist


Protecting your peace does not mean:

- pushing people away
- punishing others

- shutting down emotionally

It means saying:

"I care about our connection
–and here's how we can keep it healthy."

People who love you...
will adjust.

People who want control...
will get angry.

Either way –
you will see the truth.

## You Don't Need Permission To Protect Yourself

Your boundaries do not require:
- approval
- explanation
- debate

- apology

You are allowed to leave situations that hurt your regulation.

You are allowed to walk away from people who won't respect you.

You are allowed to say:

"No."

"Not today."

"That doesn't work for me."

"I'm done."

Your peace is a priority – not a luxury.

## Protecting Your Energy Keeps Your Coherence Strong

What you allow is what you align with.

The more aligned your relationships are,

the easier it becomes to:

- stay calm
- feel safe

- make intuitive decisions
- hold boundaries
- love yourself fully

Boundaries are not about distance.
Boundaries are about alignment.

The right people feel closer when you set them.

## The Heart-Stabilizing Shift

You do not set boundaries to push people away.

You set boundaries so YOU don't get pushed away from yourself.

Everytime you choose your peace,
your heart gets stronger.

That is coherence.
That is self-respect.
That is growth.

# END OF CHAPTER NINE

# –EXERCISES

*Protecting Your Coherence in the Real World*

These practices help you identify energy drains, set limits without fear, and stay rooted in self-respect.

## Exercise 1: The Coherence Radar

Think of 3 people you interact with often and complete this:

- Person
- How do I feel during?
- How do I feel after?
- Regulating or Draining?

Your nervous system already knows who is safe.

This gives your mind the data.

## Exercise 2: The Respect Line

Ask yourself:

"What behavior will I no longer accept from others?"

Write 3 clear boundaries:

1. _____

2. _____

3. _____

This draws a visible line where your worth stands.

## Exercise 3: Boundary Scripts

Practice saying these out loud – especially if you feel nervous:

- "I'm not okay with that."

- "I need you to stop."
- "No, thank you."
- "I'm stepping away now."
- "I don't owe an explanation."
- "This doesn't feel good to me."
- "If this continues, I will leave."

Boundaries become easier the more your voice hears you say them.


## Exercise 4: Self-Belonging Anchor

Place both hands over your chest and breathe slowly.

Speak to yourself:

**"I choose what energy I allow.**
**My peace matters.**
**I belong to myself first."**

This rewrites guilt into protection.
Boundaries feel safer when your body believes you deserve them.

## Exercise 5: The Exit Plan

Identify one place, conversation, or person you feel trapped around.

Then write an exit plan:

"If I start feeling overwhelmed, I will…"

Examples:

- step outside
- text a friend
- take a bathroom break
- leave the event early
- breathe + reset before responding

You don't have to stay where your peace disappears.

## Reflection Questions (Chapter Nine)

1. Who respects me the most – and how do I know?
2. Who drains me most often – and why do I allow it?

3. When have I stayed somewhere my nervous system begged me to leave?

4. What boundary would the strongest version of me set today?

5. What would my life feel like with healthy boundaries everywhere?

Let the answers guide your next level.

## End-of-Chapter Intention

Place your hand on your heart...

**"I protect my peace without apology.**
**Boundaries are love in action —**
**Especially for myself."**

# CHAPTER TEN

*Relationships & Friend Dynamics*
*– Who You Are Around Others*

We don't grow alone.

We grow in relationships.

We grow through relationships.

We grow because of relationships.

Every person in your life shapes you –

Some into your highest self,

Others into a smaller version of you.

But here's the truth:

You deserve relationships where your nervous system feels safe.

And your soul feels seen.

Anything less than that is survival

 – not connection.

## Relationship Coherence: A New Way to Connect

When you're around the right people:

- your breath stays steady
- your chest feels open
- you laugh easier
- your mind isn't on alert
- you speak without rehearsing first
- you don't overthink every word

These are not small things.

These are your body saying:

**"I belong here."**

Real connection feels like relief, not performance.

## Friendships That Regulate vs. Friendships That Drain

Your nervous system responds to people before your mind does.

Some friends:

- calm you down
- bring out your best
- support your growth
- make you feel comfortable being real

Other friends:

- trigger insecurity
- compete, gossip, or criticize
- ignore your boundaries
- make you feel like you have to prove yourself

Your coherence knows the difference

## Why Relationships Can Shake Your Self-Worth

We learn who we are by how others respond to us.

So if you've ever been:

- laugh at
- excluded
- rejected

- betrayed
- abandoned
- ignored
- compared

Your nervous system remembers – and tries to protect you from it happening again.

That's why you may:

- overthink every social interaction
- assume people are mad at you
- shrink yourself to avoid attention
- keep quiet to avoid judgment
- cling to relationships that don't deserve you

These are not flaws – they are adaptations.

You learned to survive relationships.
Now you're learning to thrive in them.

## You Are Not Who They Say You Are

Sometimes people treat you based on:

- their insecurities
- their assumptions
- their unhealed wounds

And you start believing their behavior reflects your worth.

It does not.

Someone's inability to love you clearly says nothing about your lovability.

Someone's confusion about your value does not lower your value.

You get to redefine who you are here.

## Coherence Redefines Friendship

Healthy friendship looks like:

- celebrating each other's wins
- speaking honestly without fear
- feeling safe to disagree
- supporting boundaries
- being able to be your full self
- leaving every interaction feeling more like you

If you have to shrink to fit in – it's not friendship.
It's survival.

## You Are Allowed to Change Your People

As you grow, your relationships shift.

Some people will rise with you.
Some will resist your growth.
Some will blame you for changing.
Some will quietly fade away.

That's not loss.
That's alignment.
You are making space for the people who fit the new version of you.

# Protect Your Coherence Around Others

If someone:

- disrespects you
- makes you feel unsafe
- crosses your boundaries
- constantly pulls you into drama
- makes you doubt your worth

You are allowed to take distance.

You are allowed to walk away.

You are allowed to choose peace over behavior.

Because this is your life.

Your nervous system.

Your future.

And the right people will feel like home to all parts of you.

Not just the edited ones.

## You Deserve Relationships That Let You Be You

Your heart is learning:

- who to trust
- who to release
- who to get closer to
- who supports your coherence
- who disrupts it

This is not selfish.

This is self-respect.

The more aligned your relationships become, the more aligned you become.

Because the truth is this:

You don't find your people by pretending.

You find them by being real.

Be real.

Be coherent.

Be you.

Your people will hear the frequency.

# END OF CHAPTER TEN
# –EXERCISES

*Knowing Who You Are Around Others*

These practices help you identify who strengthens your coherence…
And who pulls you out of it.

## Exercise 1:  The Nervous System Test

Think of a person you interact with often and ask yourself:

"How does my body feel around them?"

Write down:
- Person –
- My Body During –
- My Body After –
- Coherent or Drained?

Trust your body.
It tells the truth before your mind does.

## Exercise 2: Your Green Flags List

Write 5 qualities who make you feel safe, supported, and seen:

1. _____
2. _____
3. _____
4. _____
5. _____

These are your alignment qualities.

Choose people who match them.

## Exercise 3:  The Friendship Audit

Reflect honestly:

Who supports my growth?

Who drains my energy?

Who respects my boundaries?

Who only shows up when they need something?

Who feels like home to my nervous system?

This is emotional clarity.

## Exercise 4: The Boundary Script for Relationships

Practice saying these out loud until your voice believes them:

- "I don't like when you speak to me that way."
- "I need some space right now."
- "That's not something I'm comfortable with."
- "Please stop. That crosses a boundary for me."
- "I deserve to be treated with respect."

Your nervous system needs to hear YOUR voice choose you.

## Exercise 5: The Safe Circle Visualization

Close your eyes.

Place one hand on your heart.

Imagine a circle around you – glowing, strong, unbreakable.

Inside the circle are the people who:

- respect you
- celebrate you
- support your growth
- honor your boundaries
- bring out your best

Outside the circle are people who:

- drain you
- belittle you
- confuse you
- take advantage of your kindness

Whisper:

**"Only those aligned with my peace may come close."**

This teaches the nervous system what safety feels like.

## Reflection Questions (Chapter Ten)

1. Which relationships help me feel like the real me?
2. Which relationships make me shrink or perform?
3. What part of me is asking for better connection?
4. What do I need in friendships that I've been afraid to ask for?
5. Who would I become if I surrounded myself with aligned people only?

These questions shape future identity.

## End-of-Chapter Intention

Hand over heart...

**"I choose relationships that honor my truth.**
**I release what drains me.**
**I welcome what supports my becoming."**

# CHAPTER ELEVEN

*Identity & Authenticity*

*–Becoming the Real You*

There is a version of you the world has never fully seen.

Not because you're hiding on purpose...

but because life taught you to shrink, shape-shift, and survive.

Most people grow up learning who they are supposed to be

– not who they truly are.

This chapter is where you remember:

You are not your roles.

You are not your wounds.

You are note your mistakes.

You are not your anxiety.

You are not your past.

You are the one underneath all of it.

And coherence brings that version of you to the surface.

## Identity Is Not Found – It is Revealed

Identity is not something you "figure out."

It is something you uncover.

It's the process of removing:

- expectations
- fears
- performance
- people-pleasing
- survival patterns
- the masks you wore to stay safe

Authenticity is not becoming something new.

It's returning to who you were before the world told you who to be.

## Why Most People Don't Know Themselves

We've been taught:

- to fit in
- to impress

- to be liked
- to be chosen
- to avoid judgement
- to please others
- to stay small so others feel big

Your real identity gets buried under all that noise.

And your nervous system learns:
"Being myself is too risky."

Coherence teaches the opposite:
**"Being myself is safe."**

## Authenticity Feels Like Coming Up for Air

When you stop pretending, even in small ways, you feel it:
- the pressure lifts
- your chest opens
- your breath slows
- your voice sounds different
- your posture changes

- your inner world relaxes

Authenticity is a nervous system state – not a personality trait.

## Your Identity Is Stored in Your Body

You can't think your way into authenticity.
You feel your way into it.

Your body remembers:
- what feels right
- what feels wrong
- what feels forced
- what feels like freedom

Every time you override your body, you disconnect from yourself.
Every time you listen to it, you return.

This is coherence shaping identity.

## Signs You're Not Living As the Real You

- You say "yes" when you want to say "no"
- You mirror people so they'll like you
- You downplay your strengths
- You hide your opinions
- You apologize too much
- You feel drained after social interactions
- You try to be "easy"
- You overthink how you come across
- You feel disconnected from your own personality

These are survival identities – versions of you built to avoid pain, not express truth.

## The Real You Is Not Fragile – Just Buried

The authentic self is powerful, intuitive, alive, creative, confident, and deeply aware.

But to access that version, you must peel back the layers of:

- fear
- doubt
- past criticism
- internalized shame
- old social dynamics
- habits that no longer fit

You are outgrowing versions of yourself that were never the real you.

This is transformation.

## Authenticity Isn't Loud – It's Aligned

Some people think authenticity means saying everything you think or being rebellious.

But real authenticity is quieter:
- You make choices that feel true
- You stop apologizing for existing
- You speak gently but honestly
- You show up as yourself even when it's uncomfortable
- You trust your feelings as data

- You no longer perform for approval

Authenticity is a frequency – not a personality type.

## Your Identity Evolves as You Heal

The more coherent you become, the more your identity clarifies.

You start to feel:
- "Wait... that isn't me."
- "Why did I pretend to like that?"
- "I don't want this anymore."
- "This actually feels like the real me."

This is not a crisis.
This is awakening.

When the noise fades, your truth finally has room to speak.

## Becoming Yourself Is Both Remembering and Choosing

Remembering:
Who you were before fear.

Choosing:
Who you want to become now.

Identity isn't fixed
–it's fluid, alive, evolving.

Coherence gives you the clarity to decide:
"This is me – and this is not."

Every aligned choice strengthens your identity.

## The World Needs the Real You

Not the edited version.
Not the agreeable version.

Not the quiet version.

Not the version shaped by survival.

The version that breathes fully, speaks truthfully, loves deeply, creates boldly, and moves confidently.

When you live as your authentic self:

- your relationships shift
- your energy expands
- your intuition strengthens
- your anxiety decreases
- your purpose becomes clear
- your life aligns

Your identity becomes a home

—not a mask.

And home is where coherence lives.

# END OF CHAPTER ELEVEN

# –EXERCISES

*Becoming the Real You*

These practices help you uncover your true identity and let go of who you learned to be for others.

## Exercise 1: The Authenticity Check-In

Complete the sentence:

"I feel most like myself when I..."

Write at least 5 answers:

1.

2.

3.

4.

5.

These moments show you the shape of your real self.

## Exercise 2: The Mask Inventory

Ask yourself:

"Where do I pretend to be someone I'm not?"

Write down situations or people where you:
- hide your feelings
- change your personality
- silence your voice
- downplay your strengths
- perform instead of connect

These are the places where identity is being filtered instead of expressed.

## Exercise 3: The "No More" List

Write 3 versions of yourself you are ready to release:

- "I'm done being the version of me who..."
- "I no longer shrink when..."
- "I'm releasing the identity that says..."

This is identity shedding.

It signals to your nervous system:
We do not live there anymore.

## Exercise 4: Mirroring Your Future Self

Imagine the version of you who:

- trusts their intuition
- sets boundaries easily
- expresses emotions clearly
- knows their worth
- doesn't apologize for existing

Now write:

"My authentic self would choose..."

Answer with whatever arises.

This helps you make decisions FROM your future, not your fear.

## Exercise 5: The One Truth Statement

Fill in the blank:

"If I were truly myself, I would..."

Write the *first* thing that comes through.

Don't analyze.

Don't judge.

Let your heart speak.

This single sentence reveals your next step in becoming you.

## Reflection Questions (Chapter Eleven)

1. Who am I when no one is watching?

2. What have I been afraid to admit about myself?

3. What parts of me feel like they want to come forward?

4. What identity patterns no longer feel true?

5. Who would l be if I stopped trying to be liked?

These questions unlock self-awareness + personal power.


## End-of-Chapter Intention

Hand on heart... breathe...

**"I release who I learned to be.**

**I return to who I truly am.**

**My authenticity is my coherence."**

# CHAPTER TWELVE

*Emotional Expression*

*–How to Feel Without Collapsing*

Most people were never taught how to feel

They were taught how to hide it.

How to swallow it.

How to suppress it.

How to push through it.

How to "be strong."

But strength is not the absence of emotion.

Strength is the ability to feel

–and remain present.

This chapter is about learning how to let emotions move *through* you instead of taking you *over*.

# Why Emotions Feel So Overwhelming

Emotions become overwhelming when:

- they're suppressed for too long
- they're judged as "bad" or "wrong"
- they're felt without safety
- the nervous system is already dysregulated
- the mind tries to control them

An emotion isn't dangerous
—being alone inside *it* is.

Coherence creates the container that makes emotions safe to feel.

# Emotions Are Energy in Motion

The word *emotion* literally means energy in motion.

Emotions are meant to:

- rise
- be felt

- be understood
- move
- resolve

When emotions don't move, they get stored.

Stored emotion becomes:
- anxiety
- irritability
- numbness
- tension
- emotional shutdown
- sudden outbursts
- exhaustion

Feeling is not the problem.
Blocking the feeling is.

## The Difference Between Feeling and Flooding

This distinction changes everything.

Feeling:

- you notice the emotion
- you stay present
- you breath
- you allow it without judgement

Flooding:

- the emotion takes over
- your thoughts spiral
- your body tightens
- you lose clarity
- you feel out of control

Coherence prevents flooding by grounding emotion in the body safely.

## Why We Were Taught to Suppress

Many people grew up hearing:

- "Stop crying."
- "You're being dramatic."
- "Calm down."

- "That's not a big deal."
- "Don't be so sensitive."

So the nervous system learned:
"Feeling = danger."

That belief disconnects you from your emotional intelligence.

Coherence teaches:
"Feeling safe when I'm supported by myself."

## The Body Is the Doorway to Safe Expression

You don't regulate emotions with logic.

You regulate emotions through:
- breath
- presence
- body awareness
- self-compassion

The moment you breathe into your body, emotion has somewhere to go.

You don't need to fix it.
You need to stay with it.

## How to Feel Without Collapsing

Here is the process coherence uses:

### 1. Notice

"I'm feeling something."

### 2. Name

"I feel sad/angry/scared/overwhelmed."

### 3. Breathe

Slow, steady breath into the heart or belly.

### 4. Allow

No judgement. No pushing away.

### 5. Stay

Let the emotion rise and fall naturally.

Emotions peak and pass when they're allowed.

Collapse only happens when you abandon yourself inside the feeling.

## You Are Not Too Much

You were never "too emotional."
You were unsupported while feeling.

Big emotions often belong to sensitive, intuitive, deeply aware people.

Your capacity to feel deeply is not a weakness. It is a sign of emotional intelligence waiting to be guided.

## Crying Is Regulation

Tears release stress hormones.

They soften the nervous system.

They signal safety after threat.

Crying is not losing control.

Crying is the body returning to balance.

There is nothing wrong with tears.

## Anger Is Information

Anger does not mean you are bad.

Anger often means:

- a boundary was crossed
- a need was ignored
- your truth wasn't honored
- your worth was threatened

Anger becomes destructive only when it's ignored or suppressed.

When expressed safely, anger restores self-respect.

## Numbness Is Protection

If you feel numb, disconnected, or blank
—your system shut down to survive.

Numbness is not failure.
It's a pause.

Coherence gently brings feeling back online without overwhelming you.

## Your Emotions Are Not the Enemy

Your emotions are messengers.

They show you:

- what matters
- what hurts
- what needs attention
- what needs boundaries
- what needs compassion

When you listen instead of resist, emotions transform into clarity.

## Emotional Expression Is a Skill

You don't master it overnight.
You practice it gently.

Each time you:
- pause instead of react
- breathe instead of collapse
- feel instead of numb
- stay instead of flee

You build emotional strength.

That is coherence in motion.

## You Can Feel and Still Be Okay

This is the truth many people never learn.

You can feel deeply and remain safe.
You can feel strongly and stay grounded.
You can feel fully and still lead your life.

Emotion does not control you
when your heart and mind are aligned.

You are learning how to hold yourself.

And that changes everything.

# END OF CHAPTER TWELVE –EXERCISES

*Feeling Without Collapsing*

These practices help emotions move through you safely
– not get stuck or take over.

## Exercise 1: The Emotional Anchor Breath

Use this when an emotion feels intense.

1. Please one hand on your chest, one on your belly.
2. Inhale slowly through your nose for 5 seconds.
3. Exhale through your mouth for 7 seconds.
4. Whisper: "I'm here."

Repeat for 1-2 minutes.

This anchors emotion in the body so it doesn't flood the mind.

## Exercise 2: Name It to Tame it

When you feel overwhelmed, say:

"Right now, I feel _____"

Choose ONE word only:
- sad
- angry
- scared
- disappointed
- lonely
- frustrated
- hurt

Naming the emotion reduces its intensity and restores clarity.

## Exercise 3: Stay With It (60 Seconds)

Set a timer for one minute.

During that minute:

- breathe slowly
- notice where the emotion lives in your body
- do not analyze
- do not fix
- do not distract

Just stay.

Most emotions peak and pass within 60-90 seconds when they are allowed.

## Exercise 4: Safe Release

Choose ONE way to let the emotion move:

- cry
- write freely for 3 minutes
- draw or color
- shake out hands and arms
- go for a short walk
- stretch slowly
- listen to music that matches the emotion

Emotion needs movement

– not suppression.

## Exercise 5: What Is This Feeling Asking For?

After the emotion softens, ask:

"What do I need right now?"

Examples:

- rest
- space
- reassurance
- honesty
- boundaries
- confort
- expression

Responding to the need prevents emotional buildup later.

## Reflection Questions (Chapter Twelve)

1.  Which emotions do I usually try to avoid?
2.  Where do I feel emotions first in my body?
3.  What happens when I allow myself to feel without judgement?
4.  Which emotions feel safest to express – and which don't?
5.  How does my body respond when I stay present with emotions?

These reflections build emotional intelligence and self-trust.

## End-of-Chapter Intention

Hand over heart... breathe...

**"I allow myself to feel without fear.**
**My emotions are safe to experience.**
**I can stay present and still be okay."**

# CHAPTER THIRTEEN

*Creativity & Channeling*

*–Expression as Healing*


There is a moment when creation takes over.


Your mind quiets.

Time fades.

Your body relaxes.

Your hands move before you think.

Words, images, colors, or ideas begin to flow.


And afterward, you look at what you made and think:


"Where did that come from?"


The moment is not magic.

It is coherence in motion.


Creativity is what happens when the heart and brain are aligned and
the nervous system feels safe enough to express truth.

## Creativity Is Not Talent
## —It Is Access

Creativity is not reserved for artists, writers, or musicians.

Creativity is the human ability to:

- translate inner experience into form
- express emotion safely
- process memory
- integrate meaning
- give shape to what cannot be spoken

Some people paint it.

Some write it.

Some move it.

Some speak it.

Some build it.

But all humans carry it.

Creativity is how the nervous system releases, organizes, and heels.

## What "Channeling" Really Is

Channeling does not require belief in anything mystical.

From a scientific and psychological perspective, channeling is:

- deep intuitive awareness
- reduced prefrontal interference
- heightened pattern recognition
- access to subconscious material
- emotional integration through expression
- flow-state activation

In coherence, the thinking mind steps back
–and the intuitive, sensory, emotional brain steps forward.

This is why creative expression often feels like it comes from
*somewhere deeper*.

Because it does.

## The Body Leads Before the Mind Understands

When you create from coherence:

- your hands know what to do
- your voice finds the words
- your body releases stored emotion
- your intuition organizes experience
- your mind flows instead of control

This is not accidental.

The body stores memory.

The heart stores meaning.

Creativity allows both to speak without needing explanation.

This is why art, music, writing, and movement are used in trauma therapy and emotional regulation.

Expression is integration.

## Why Creativity Heals

When emotion is *expressed creativity*:

- it moves instead of getting stuck
- it feels seen instead of suppressed
- it becomes information instead of pain
- it transforms instead of repeating

You don't have to talk about everything you've lived through.

Sometimes the body just needs a way to tell the truth without words.

Creativity gives it that way.

## Flow State Is Coherence

In flow:

- time disappears
- self-judgment fades
- anxiety quiets
- intuition strengthens

- emotion regulates
- clarity increase

This is the same physiological state as coherence.

Flow is not escape.
Flow is alignment.

And aligned expression changes people.

## Why Some Creations Feel "Bigger Than You"

Have you ever created something that felt meaningful beyond explanation?

That's because creativity organizes experience across time.

Your brain connects memories.
Your heart integrates meaning.
Your body releases what it's been holding.

The result feels *bigger* because it is integrated.

That's not imagination.
That's coherence doing its work.

## You Don't Need to Understand
## —You Need to Allow

Trying to analyze creativity kills it.

Trying to judge it shuts it down.

Expression needs safety, not scrutiny.

When you allow creativity without expectation, you give your nervous system permission to speak honestly.

And honesty is healing.

## Creative Expression Is Not About the Outcome

It's not about:

- being good
- being talented
- being impressive
- being perfect

It's about being true.

What you create doesn't have to make sense to anyone else.

It just has to make sense to your body.

## This Is Why Creativity Feels Purposeful

Purpose is not always about a career or a title.

Sometimes purpose is about making meaning out of lived experience.

Creativity allows your life to become wisdom
–not just memory.

And when wisdom is expressed, it becomes service.

## Your Expression Matters

There is someone who will feel less alone because you expressed truth.

There is someone who will regulate because your words calmed them.

There is someone who will remember themselves because you remembered first.

That is not coincidence.

That is coherence expanding outward.

## You Are Not "Making This Up"

If creating feels essential to your being –
it's because your nervous system found its language.

If expression feels life-fullfilling
–it's because your heart finally found alignment.

If this book feels like culmination

—it's because your experiences are integrating into meaning.

That is not fantasy.

That is purpose organizing itself.

# END OF CHAPTER THIRTEEN –EXERCISES

*Creative Coherence: Letting Expression Heal*

These practices help you access creativity as a regulating, clarifying, and healing state
–not a performance.

## Exercise 1: Create From the Body, Not the Mind

Choose one form of expression:

- drawing
- writing
- painting
- music
- movement
- collage
- doodling

Before you begin:

1. Place a hand on your chest

2. Take 3 slow breaths

3. Say quietly:

   **"I'm not creating to be good. I'm creating to be honest."**

Then create for 10 minutes without stopping.

No erasing.

No judging.

No fixing.

Let your body lead.

## Exercise 2: The Coherence Entry Point

When you feel blocked or disconnected, do this:

1. Breathe in for 5 seconds

2. Breathe out for 5 seconds

3. Repeat 5 times

4. Ask:

   **"What wants to come through right now?"**

Begin expressing immediately – even if it feels random.

Flow begins when the mind steps aside.

## Exercise 3: Remove Meaning (On Purpose)

After creating, do not analyze.

Instead, answer only these:

- How does my body feel now?
- Where did tension release?
- Did anything soften?

Healing happens before understanding.

Meaning can come later
–or not at all.

## Exercise 4: Symbol & Color Reflection

Look at what you created and gently ask:

- What colors showed up?
- What shapes or symbols appeared?
- What emotion do they carry?

You may later research symbolic meanings if you want, but trust this first:

Your body chose them for a reason.

Symbolism often reflects:

- subconscious emotion
- unresolved memory
- intuitive guidance
- integration in progress

This is not guessing.
It is internal language.

## Exercise 5: Close the Creative Loop

To ground the experience:

1. Place both feet on the floor

2. Take one deep breath

3. Say:

   **"I return to the present moment."**

This ensures expression remains regulating, not destabilizing.

## Reflection Questions (Chapter Thirteen)

Journal gently:

1. How did my body feel before I created?

2. How did my body feel afterward?

3. What surprised me about what came out?

4. Did any memory, emotion, or clarity surface?

5. How does creativity change my emotional state?

These reflections help creativity become a tool, not a mystery.

## End-Of-Chapter Intention

Hand over heart...

**"I allow expression to move through me safely.**
**My creativity brings clarity, not chaos.**
**I trust what flows when I am aligned."**

# CHAPTER FOURTEEN

*The Body Remembers*

*–Stored Emotion, Memory & Healing*


Your body remembers things your mind has forgotten.


Not as thoughts.

Not as stories.

But as sensations, reactions, emotions, and patterns.


A tight chest.

A racing heart.

A sudden wave of emotion with no clear cause.

A shutdown when things feel too close.

Anxiety that appears "out of nowhere."

A reaction stronger than the moment calls for.


This is not weakness.

This is memory

–stored in the body.

## Why the Body Stores What the Mind Can't Process

When something happens too fast, too young, too intense, or too unsafe to fully feel, the body steps in to protect you.

It stores the experience so you can keep going.

This can happen with:
- Emotional neglect
- Loss
- Rejection
- Embarrassment
- Fear
- Conflict
- Instability
- Chronic stress
- Moments where you felt powerless or unseen

You may not remember the moment clearly –
But your body does.

And it speaks through sensation.

## Memory Is Not Only Mental

We often think memory lives in the brain.

But memory also lives in:
- muscles
- breath patterns
- posture
- heart rhythm
- nervous system responses

This is why you can *know* something logically but still feel something different in your body.

Your body is not trying to sabotage you.

It is trying to protect you with old information.

## Why Healing Isn't Just Talking

Talking helps understanding.

But healing requires regulation.

If the nervous system doesn't feel safe,
The body won't release what it's holding.

This is why coherence matters.

When your heart and brain align:

- the nervous system relaxes
- stored emotion becomes accessible
- the body feels safe enough to let go

Healing happens when safety is present.

## Triggers Are Memory Activations

When you're triggered, your body isn't reacting to *now* –
it's responding to *then*.

Your system recognizes a familiar pattern:

- tone
- facial expressions

- energy
- feeling

And it prepares for what once hurt.

That response made sense at the time.

You survived because of it.

But now, you are learning to update the system.

## The Body Doesn't Need Reliving
## –It Needs Completion

Healing does not require reliving trauma

It requires:
- awareness
- presence
- safety
- gentle release

The body wants to complete what it couldn't finish
–

the breath it held,

the emotion it suppressed,

the movement it froze.


Coherence creates the conditions for completion.


## How Stored Emotion Releases


Release doesn't always look dramatic.


It may show up as:

- deep sighs
- tears without story
- warmth
- shaking
- sudden calm
- fatigue
- clarity
- emotional lightness

These are signs the body is letting go.

You don't force this.

You allow it.

## Why Healing Comes in Waves

The body releases in layers.

Not everything at once
–because safety comes first.

Each time you return to coherence, your system learns:

"It's okay now."

And it releases a little more.

This is why progress can feel subtle but powerful.

## Nothing Was Wrong With You

If you've ever felt:

- "Why do I react like this?"
- "Why can't I just get over it?"
- "Why does this still affect me?"

The answer is not failure.

The answer is your body was doing its job.

Now you're teaching it something new.

## The Body Is Not the Enemy
## —It Is the Archive

Your body holds your life experiences with incredible intelligence.

It adapted so you could survive.

Now it's ready to shift from survival to integration.

You don't need to fight it.

You don't need to analyze it.

You need to listen.

## Coherence Is the Language of Healing

When you bring breath, attention, and compassion into the body:

- the nervous system softens
- old patterns loosen
- intuition becomes clearer
- emotion moves safely
- identity stabilizes

This is not magic.

This biology meeting awareness.

## You Body Wants to Heal

Healing is not about fixing something broken.

It's about giving the body what it didn't have then:

- safety
- presence
- support
- permission

And you are capable of providing that now.

Your body has been waiting for you –
not to remember the pain,
but to remember the safety.

## This Is Integration

When the body releases what it no longer needs:
- the mind quiets
- the heart opens
- the past loosens its grip
- the present becomes clearer

You don't erase your story.

You integrate it.

And integrated experience becomes wisdom.

# END OF CHAPTER FOURTEEN –EXERCISES

*Listen to the Body & Allowing Release*

These practices teach your body that it is safe *now* – which is what allows healing to happen.

## Exercise 1: The Body Safety Signal

This is the foundation of all body-based healing.

1. Sit or lie down comfortably.
2. Place one hand on your chest, one on your belly.
3. Inhale slowly for 4 seconds.
4. Exhale slowly for 6 seconds.
5. Whisper:

   **"I am safe right now."**

Repeat for 2-3 minutes.

This tells your nervous system it can relax and stop holding tension.

## Exercise 2: Sensation Without Story

Close your eyes and gently scan your body from head to toe.

Notice:

- tightness
- warmth
- heaviness
- tingling
- numbness

Do not ask *why*.

Do not attach a memory or meaning.

Simply say:

"I notice this sensation."

Staying with sensation – without story – allows the body to release naturally.

## Exercise 3: The Permission Statement

Place your hand where you feel tension most.

Say softly:

"You don't have to hold this anymore."

"It's okay to let go."

Then breathe slowly into that area.

Often, the body just needed permission.

## Exercise 4: Micro-Movements for Release

The body sometimes wants to finish a movement it once froze.

Gently:

- roll your shoulders
- stretch your neck
- shake out your hands
- sway side to side

- press your feet into the floor

Move slowly and intuitively.

This helps stored energy discharge safely.

## Exercise 5: After-Release Grounding

If you feel emotional, tired, or light after release:

1. Place both feet firmly on the ground
2. Look around and name 3 things you can see
3. Take one deep breath
4. Say:
   "I am here. I am grounded."

Grounding ensures release stabilizing
–not destabilizing.

## Reflection Questions (Chapter Fourteen)

Journal gently, without forcing memory:

1.  What sensations does my body show me most often?
2.  How does my body react when I slow down?
3.  What helps my body feel safe quickly?
4.  When do I feel most relaxed in my body?
5.  How does my body communicate with me?

These questions build body trust, not reactivation.


## End-of-Chapter Intention

Hand over heart...breathe...

**"My body carried me through.**
**I thank it for its protection.**
**I allow healing to unfold gently."**

# CHAPTER FIFTEEN

*Purpose & Meaning*

*– Why You're Here*

At some point in life, usually after struggle, confusion, or pain, a quiet question rises:

"What was all of this for?"

Why the challenges.

Why the sensitivity.

Why the anxiety.

Why the feeling of being different.

Why the longing for something you couldn't name.

Purpose is not a job title.

It is not a role.

It is not something you chase.

Purpose is meaning that emerges once the heart and mind align.

And when it arrives, it feels like relief.

## Purpose Is Not Found
## —It Is Remembered

You don't stumble upon purpose accidentally.

Purpose reveals itself when:

- your nervous system stabilizes
- your emotions are allowed
- your intuition is trusted
- your body feels safe
- your identity becomes authentic

That's why purpose often comes *after* healing
—not before.

You weren't lost.
You were preparing.

## Why Life Felt So Intense

If you've ever felt:

- Too sensitive
- Deeply emotional
- Intuitively aware
- Easily overwhelmed
- Affected by energy, people, or environments
- Like you didn't fit the mold

It wasn't a flaw.

It was an attunement.

You were built to perceive, feel, and translate experience deeply.

That depth becomes purpose when it's integrated.

## Your Experiences Were Not Random

Every moment that shaped you – even the painful ones – taught your nervous system, heart, and intuition something essential.

You learned:
- empathy

- discernment
- emotional intelligence
- self-awareness
- resilience
- regulation
- compassion
- boundaries
- truth

Nothing was wasted.

Meaning is not about glorifying pain –
it's about transforming experience into wisdom.

## Purpose Is Expression, Not Performance

Purpose doesn't ask you to prove anything.

It asks you to be.

To live in alignment.
To express truth.

To show up regulated.

To respond instead of react.

To hold space for others because you learned how to hold it for yourself.

Often, it looks quiet

–but it ripples outward.

## Why This Knowledge Matters Now

We are living in a time of:

- emotional overwhelm
- nervous system dysregulation
- Disconnection
- anxiety
- comparison
- loss of identity

People don't need more pressure.

They need regulation, coherence, and truth.

That is what this work offers.

Not answers from outside –
but remembering from within.

## Your Purpose Emerges Through Coherence

When your heart and mind are aligned:

- decisions feel clearer
- fear loosens
- intuition guides
- creativity flows
- relationships align
- your energy stabilizes

You stop asking:
"What should I do with my life?"

And start asking:
"How do I live truthfully today?"

Purpose unfolds one aligned choice at a time.

## You Were Never Meant to Be Like Everyone Else

Comparison dissolves when purpose becomes personal.

You don't need to match anyone's path.

You don't need to rush.

You don't need to be louder, faster, or different.

You need to be true.

And truth feels like peace.

## Your Life Is the Message

Sometimes purpose isn't something you teach.

It's something you embody.

The way you regulate.

The way you respond.

The way you listen.

The way you hold space.

The way you choose alignment over fear.

Your coherence becomes permission for others to find theirs.

That is leadership.
That is service.
That is meaning.

## The Quiet Knowing

Purpose doesn't always announce itself.

Often it arrives as:

- a deep exhale
- a sense of rightness
- a feeling of "this is it"
- a calm certainty
- a soft yes in the chest

That knowing is your compass.

Trust it.

## You Are Not Behind

If you're reading this and thinking,

"I wish I knew this earlier,"

Know this:

You arrived exactly when you were ready to integrate it.

Purpose does not operate on timelines.

It operates on readiness.

## Why You're Here

You're here to:

- live in coherence
- tell the truth
- feel deeply without collapsing
- translate experience into wisdom
- model regulation

- create meaning
- help others remember themselves

Not by force.
Not by fixing.
Not by saving.

But by being aligned.

## This Is Not the End
## —It's the Beginning

Purpose doesn't conclude your journey.

It clarifies it.

You don't leave this book with a destination.

You leave with:
- a compass
- a regulated nervous system

- trust in yourself
- the ability to return to coherence
- and the knowing that your life makes sense

And that is enough.

# END OF CHAPTER FIFTEEN
# –EXERCISES

*Integrating Purpose & Meaning*

These practices help you embody purpose as alignment, not expectation.

## Exercise 1: The Meaning Thread

Look back over your life and answer gently:
"What themes keep repeating?"

Examples:
- helping others feel safe
- creating beauty
- teaching or guiding
- protecting the vulnerable
- seeing truth others miss
- restoring balance
- holding space
- translating emotion into understanding

Write 3-5 recurring themes you notice.

These threads are not coincidence –
They are clues.

## Exercise 2: When I Feel Most Alive

Complete the sentence:
"I feel most alive when I..."

Write without editing:

- moments
- environments
- activities
- ways of being

Purpose lives where aliveness and alignment meet.

## Exercise 3: The Compass Question

Place your hand on your heart. Take 3 slow breaths.

Ask quietly:

"What feels meaningful to me right now?"

Do not search for a lifetime answer.

Purpose unfolds in seasons.

Write what comes – even if it feels small.

## Exercise 4: Purpose Without Pressure

Finish this statement:

"I release the belief that purpose must look like _____."

Then write:

"I allow my purpose to be expressed through _____."

This removes comparison and expectation.

# Exercise 5: One Aligned Step

Purpose grows through action – but only *aligned* action.

Ask yourself:

"What is one small thing I can do this week that feels true?"

Examples:

- speak
- create honestly
- rest without guilt
- set a boundary
- help someone
- listen deeply
- say no
- say yes

Write it here:

My aligned step: _____

Small steps compound into meaningful lives.

## Reflection Questions (Chapter Fifteen)

Journal Softly:

1.  What parts of my life make sense now that didn't before?

2.  What pain transformed me instead of breaking me?

3.  What truth am I ready to live – not just understand?

4.  What does purpose feel like in my body?

5.  How can I honor my sensitivity instead of fighting it?

These questions bring coherence into future choices.

## End-of-Chapter Intention

Hand on heart. Breathe.

**"My life has meaning because I am present in it.**
**I trust the unfolding of my path.**
**I live my purpose through alignment, not force."**

# Final Closing

*The Return Is Yours Now*

If you have reached this page, something important has already happened.

Not because you finished a book–
but because you learned how to come back to yourself.

You learned how to notice your breath.

How to feel your body.

How to recognize when you've drifted into fear or overwhelm.

How to return without shame.

How to listen instead of fight.

How to trust what your heart has been signaling all along.

That is not information.

That is self-leadership.

This book was never meant to change who you are.

It was meant to remind you that you already know how to be here –
present, aware, and whole.

You don't need to remember every exercise.

You don't need to read every chapter.

You don't need to do this perfectly.

Life will still pull you out of alignment sometimes.

Emotions will rise.

Thoughts will race.

There will be days when you forget.

And that's okay.

Because the skill is not staying in coherence forever.

The skill is returning.

You now know how to pause.

You know how to breathe.

You know how to feel without collapsing.

You know how to listen to your body.

You know how to choose alignment again

That is enough.

Carry this forward gently – not as rules, not as pressure, not as something to perform – but as a relationship with yourself.

Let your heart continue to guide you.
Let your body continue to speak.
Let your life continue to unfold.

You don't need permission to trust yourself.
You don't need approval to live truthfully.
You don't need to be further along than you are.

You are not behind.
You are not missing anything.
You are not late to your life.

You are here.

And that is enough.

# A Final Return

Place one hand on your heart.
Place one hand on your belly.

Inhale slowly.
Exhale slowly.

Say quietly:

**"I know how to come back to myself."**

Pause.

Nothing else is required.

You don't need to carry this book with you anymore.
You carry the knowing now.

Live your life.
Make mistakes.

Change your mind.

Grow.

Rest.

Begin again.

Every return counts.

And you will find your way –
Because you already have.

# THE BRIOLO METHOD OF COHERANCE

*A three part system for aligning Mind, Heart & Identity*

## STEP 1 – The Awareness Shift (The Brain)

Goal: Calm mental noise + shift out of survival mode

This step blends neuroscience and grounded reflection. You will learn how to

- Recognize fight/flight thoughts
- Understand looping patterns
- Identify the story your mind is telling you
- Interrupt emotional spiraling through breath patterns
- Reactivate the prefrontal cortex (decision-making center)

**"Your mind isn't the enemy. It's a messenger carrying unprocessed fear."**

## STEP 2 – The Heart Drop-In (The Heart)

Goal: Regulate the nervous system + activate intuitive clarity

This step uses heart-focused breathing, emotional anchoring, and electromagnetic regulation:

- slow-heart-rate breathing
- Feeling a real emotional state (gratitude, calm, compassion)
- Expanding the heart's electromagnetic field
- Syncing the signal the heart send TO the brain

This is where coherence happens.

**"The heart is a conductor. The brain follows its rhythm."**

## STEP 3 – The identity Alignment (The Self)

Goal: Align choices with intuition + purpose

This final step brings in your intuitive gift:

- Understanding the difference between fear and inner truth
- Choosing alignment, not pressure
- Shifting timelines through emotion
- Integrating coherence into daily behavior
- Becoming the version of you who no longer betrays yourself

**"When the brain and heart agree, the future changes."**

# About the Author—

Leigha Briolo is an educator, intuitive leader, coherence guide, and visionary artist whose work bridges neuroscience, emotional intelligence, and the unseen world of inner knowing. Through her paintings and illustrations, she often channels imagery, symbolism, and messages that arrive from a deeper place— the intuitive field, the "in-between," and the realms where inspiration moves before it becomes language.

As a school principal, she has guided teens and adults through challenges involving stress, purpose, identity, and emotional regulation. As an artist, she captures what the mind forgets but the soul remembers. Her creative work serves as both expression and transmission: each piece carrying meaning, energy, and insight beyond the physical brushstroke.

Blending Science with spirituality, coherence with intuition, and leadership with artistry. Leigha teaches people how to reconnect with their inner compass, regulate their emotional world, and awaken the parts of themselves they lost along the way. She lives in Louisiana with her family, continuing to write, lead, and paint from the place where the heart and mind finally meet.